A HANNES BOK TREASURY

FOREWORD BY RAY BRADBURY

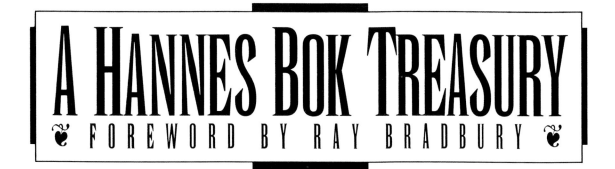

A HANNES BOK TREASURY
❦ FOREWORD BY RAY BRADBURY ❦

Edited and with an Introduction by
Stephen D. Korshak

Underwood-Miller
Novato, California
Lancaster, Pennsylvania

A Hannes Bok Treasury
ISBN 0-88733-158-0 (softcover edition)
ISBN 0-88733-157-2 (cloth edition)

Jacket design by Arnie Fenner
Book design: Underwood-Miller
Printed in the United States of America
All Rights Reserved

A second collection of Hannes Bok's artwork is being readied for publication. Anyone with information about original Bok artwork should contact the editor: Steve Korshak, 2345 Sand Lake Road, Suite 120, Orlando, FL 32809.

Library of Congress Cataloging-in-Publication Data
    A Hannes Bok treasury/edited by Stephen D. Korshak.
        Includes bibliographic references.
        ISBN 0-88733-157-2: $29.95 —ISBN 0-88733-158-0: $17.95
        1. Bok, Hannes, 1914-1964 —Themes, motives. 2. Science fiction —Illustrations. I. Bok, Hannes, 1914-1964. II. Korshak, Stephen D.
        NC975.5.B63A4 1993   93-16945
        741.6′52′092—dc20   CIP

To my friend

BOB WEINBERG

*Art historian, eminent collector, colleague, whose effort
in bringing about this book should not go unnoticed*

Hannes Bok (1914–1964)
An early photograph

HANNES BOK REMEMBERED

by Ray Bradbury

The exact date on which Hannes Bok arrived at the Little Brown Room of Clifton's cafeteria in Los Angeles is lost long in the past. I would guess shortly before I graduated from High School in June, 1938, but others must answer to this. I only recall the explosion, for that was what it was, when I first saw Hannes' work. Looking back from this great distance, it is hard to see why the explosion was so devastating. I imagine some of it was meeting a real live artist face-to-face. Plus the imaginative and rhythmic quality of Bok's work. Why we love what we love in art will always remain personal and mysterious. I only knew that I wanted to own some of his temperas, but there was little chance of that. I was flat broke, and at least a year away from selling newspapers on a street corner. I contented myself with just being around Hannes, listening to him talk about art and artists, illustrators and books, chief among them being, at that time, Maxfield Parrish.

All that I can truly remember about those years, was that Hannes taught me to play chess and that when it came time for me to take the Greyhound Bus to New York City for the First World Science-Fiction Convention, I offered to be Hannes' agent to the science-fiction and fantasy magazines. Our goal: to get him hired as cover and inside illustrator to *Astounding*, *Thrilling Wonder*, or *Weird Tales*. Forrest J Ackerman paid my bus fare and for five dollars a week I stayed in New York at the Sloane House YMCA. Bok had his works mailed on for my trudge around the editorial offices.

I showed Hannes' work to a hundred people at the First World Science-Fiction Convention. Everyone responded. Everyone, that is, except the editors. John W. Campbell, Leo Margulies, and a half dozen others, confessioned admiration. But only one, Farnsworth Wright, at *Weird Tales*, constantly shaken by Parkinson's Disease, took one look and said: Yes! I almost collapsed with relief. But there was the simple mad fact, I could *not* telephone Hannes to tell him the news. Who, in those days, had money for long-distance calls!?

From New York City I took the Greyhound Bus through upper Illinois, stopping over at my hometown Waukegan, long enough to show all my relatives I was poverty-stricken, and then pushed on to Seattle, to deliver in person the good news to Hannes that he was wanted in Manhattan, if only by *Weird Tales,* at twenty-five or thirty dollars per cover. Hannes left for New York a few weeks later and stayed there, as far as I know, for the rest of his life.

I still have dozens of his sketches, and a half dozen of his tempera paintings. They can be found around my several work desks, fifty years after our first, amiable collision. I look at them with a fond sadness, for I would have wished for Hannes the same fame that came to another close friend of the same period—Ray Harryhausen. But Ray got out there in the traffics, selling himself, carrying and steering his foot-high dinosaurs around the studios. Today there are Harryhausen film festivals all across the world.

And perhaps one day, why not? someone might grab onto a series of Bok's paintings or ink sketches, and write a children's book to fit. My old dream for Hannes would then at last come true. May it happen.

RAY BRADBURY
Los Angeles, California

ACKNOWLEDGMENTS

The editor wishes to commend the following people for extraordinary help and warm support in the preparation of this volume:

Forrest J Ackerman for great assistance in providing the names and addresses of otherwise unknown Bok collectors;

Rory Cassidy and Herb Hiestand who put words into deeds;

Lester del Ray for his patient advice in time of need;

Gerry de la Ree whose great series of science-fiction artbooks and whose art collection were a constant source of inspiration;

Alex Eisenstein and Ben Indick for providing me helpful materials;

Sam Moskowitz and Tom Goldwasser for their helpful critiques of my first draft;

Rah Hoffman for allowing me to examine his previously unpublished correspondence and for his helpful comments;

Lisa Lefkowitz whose insights into the structure and requirements of an artbook were most illuminating to a first-time artbook author;

Barry Levin of Barry Levin Books for advising me of the existence of Bok's notebooks;

Dean Mouscher whose editing skills are second to none;

Gene Nigra for graciously providing so much of his original artwork for reproductions;

Clarence Peacock the "keeper of the flame";

Maury Barlow Pepin whose restoration work will help keep Bok's artwork alive for future generations;

Emil Petaja whose biography of Bok and personal friendship with him are legendary; and

Darrell Richardson for providing me helpful materials; and

Elise Levy Bloom;   Jill Burbidge;

Mike Creamer;   Eva Eder;

A very special thanks to some additional people who were instrumental in this book:

Chuck Miller and Tim Underwood, my publishers, whose love of Bok made this book a reality;

Erle Melvin Korshak, my father, whose exquisite line of hard cover specialty press books, Shasta Books, was a constant reminder that good taste is timeless and without whose help in conceiving, organizing and promoting this book it would never have happened; and

Alma Korshak, my loving wife, whose appreciation of Bok's artwork and knowledge of his importance gave her the patience that she had in supporting my endeavors with this book.

CHRONOLOGY

1914 July 2nd. Born Wayne Woodard in Kansas City, Missouri

1927 Bok reads 3rd installment of *Amazing Stories* with A. Merritt story (July, 1927), "The Moon Pool"

1932 Graduate of Duluth (Minn.) High—Departs for Seattle

1934 (December, 1934–January, 1935) Fantasy Magazine, first appearance of Hans Bok, publication of linoleum block cover to *Cosmos*, a 17-part science-fiction story signed "Bok"

1936 Publication of artwork for Petaja's BRIEF CANDLE

1937 (or 1938) Moves to Los Angeles

1938 Works on fanzine art for Bradbury's *Futuria Fantasia*

1938 Returns to Seattle—paints "Ase on the Hillock"

1939 First professional cover for *Weird Tales*—"Hannes Bok" born. Moves to New York City, 116 West 109th Street (December, 1939)

1942 Publication of first story "Alien Vibration"—in *Future Fiction*. Publication of Novel "Starstone World"–1942 in *Science-Fiction Quarterly*. Publication of "The Sorcerers Ship" Dec. 1942 in *Unknown Worlds*.

1945 Lithographs "The Power Series"

1945 January 2 through January 13 one-man exhibition at Ferragil Art Gallery, New York

1946 Illustrates and completes the unfinished novels "THE FOX WOMAN" and "THE BLACK WHEEL" of A. Merritt—paints "Skull-Face"

1948 Publication of "The Blue Flamingo" in January, 1948, *Startling Stories* (appeared in late 1947)

1948 Paints "Slaves of Sleep"

1949 Bok attends his first and only World Science-Fiction Convention, Cincinnati (September 3-5)

1950 Draws "Pickman's Model"

1953 Presented the first Hugo as Best Artist by vote of science-fiction fans

1954 Leaves, on a full-time basis, the science-fiction/fantasy illustration field

1963 Paints last piece in the field—Cover for *The Magazine of Fantasy & Science-Fiction* "A Rose for Ecclesiastes"

1964 April 11th Hannes Bok dies of an apparent heart attack

Introduction

by Stephen D. Korshak

When Hannes Bok arrived in New York in 1939, the golden age of American illustration had passed. The great illustrators Howard Pyle, N.C. Wyeth and Maxfield Parrish had left the scene. Illustrators were no longer independent Artists with complete control of their work; their art was now subservient to the advertising and marketing whims of editors and publishers.[1]

The illustration field of 1939 was populated by pulp magazines—inexpensive publications printed on cheap, uncoated paper with garish color covers and sketchy line drawings inside. They were sold on newsstands and were devoted, for the most part, to science-fiction, westerns, detective stories, and the like.

For any artist to succeed under such circumstances was difficult. But for a self-taught artist with a totally uncompromising spirit to specialize in the fringe area of fantasy/science-fiction and hope for success seemed foolhardy. That Hannes Bok could transcend these limitations and produce sublime art was a testament to his genius.

Bok was born Wayne Woodard in Kansas City, Missouri on July 2, 1914, the youngest of four children. His parents divorced when he was five and his mother moved to Seattle, leaving her children in the custody of a strict, uncompromising father. When Bok's father remarried, it was to a woman with views similar to his own; together they attempted to discourage young Wayne from becoming an artist.

Wayne Woodard's relationship with his father was apparently so bitter that after graduation from high school in Duluth, Minnesota, he left home and severed all ties with him. In 1932 he joined his mother in Seattle and sometime thereafter renamed himself Hans Bok.[2] Eventually in 1939 with the publication of his first professional illustration, his name took its final form, Hannes Bok. Robert A. W. Lowndes, Bok's friend, claims that the etymology of the name stems from Bok's interest in Johann Sebastian Bach.[3]

Unable to procure employment upon his arrival in Seattle in 1932 during the height of the Depression, Bok used the next few years to educate himself as an artist. To buttress two years of art in high school, he immersed himself in the Seattle museums, libraries and book shops. During this same period of time Bok and many of his contemporaries began to delve more and more into the world of their own imaginations. Professional magazines specializing in science-fiction and fantasy had begun to appear in the 1920's. By the early 1930's many of the fan readers began to form clubs and publish amateur magazines of their own. By the late 1930's they had organized large-scale meetings or conventions. Bok had first been attracted to this movement at the age of twelve after reading an installment of A. Merritt's *The Moon Pool* in *Amazing Stories*. Later Bok claimed that the illustrations of that story by the great science-fiction artist Frank R. Paul had inspired his decision to be an artist.[4]

Bok attempted several times to submit portfolios of work to the pulp magazines, first in 1932 and again in 1934. His fan art first appeared in 1935 as the "linoleum block" cover to *Cosmos*, a 17-part science-fiction serial published as part of a fan magazine. His first major project from that time period consisted of ten primitive illustrations for *Brief Candle* a mimeographed book of poems by his friend and later biographer, Emil Petaja.

In 1938, after Bok's mother lost her job and his rent was increased, he moved in with Petaja in Los Angeles. There Bok met another fantasy fan, Ray Bradbury, who set Bok to work that year on his own fan magazine *Futuria Fantasia*. Bok returned to Seattle that same year and found employment with the art division of the government's Works Projects Administration (WPA). Here he was provided an opportunity to paint murals on public buildings and to meet artists of the caliber of Morris Graves and Mark Tobey.

The culmination of Bok's artistic education was a visit to his mentor Maxfield Parrish.[5] In *And Flights of Angels*, Bok's biographer, Petaja, maintains that several visits occurred although the exact dates are not known.[6]

In 1988, Erle Korshak and I purchased from Bok's estate two Parrish sketches given to Bok by Parrish. One, "Twilight," had been published in the Brown and Bigelow Calendar of 1937 and the other, "The Glen," had appeared in 1938. This, in conjunction with certain Parrish theories discussed in Bok's notebooks of 1932–1935 and the growing influence of Parrish's ideas and techniques on Bok's art during this period leads us to assume the personal visit or visits occurred within a few years before or after 1939.[7]

Bok's notebooks make clear two of Parrish's influences: Parrish's concept of Dynamic Symmetry and his technique of glazing. In a 1928 letter, Parrish described what dynamic symmetry meant to him:

> "Of late years I have been doing all my work on a layout, so to speak, of Dynamic Symmetry, a rediscovery on the part of Jay Hambridge of the old Greek method of making rectangles. Those familiar with this method consider that these dynamic rectangles are far more pleasing than just arbitrary rectangles, and not only that, but by their subdivisions they permit every feature of the picture to be part of the whole panel. If done with intelligence there is a certain balance to the design which is of great value..."[8]

This elaborate system of designing with rectangles is what gives such great harmony to a picture like Parrish's "Daybreak." Pages from Bok's notebook (*plates I&II*), show Bok's restatement of Parrish's theory and his own ideas on how to use other patterns to obtain such harmony in different ways.

A close examination of the Parrish "rough" for "Twilight" (*plate III*) , reveals extensive use of lines throughout the piece. Perhaps Parrish was demonstrating dynamic symmetry, lighting, perspective, or some similar concept to the young Bok.

Parrish's technique of glazing also began to make its way into Bok's artwork during the 1932–1938 period. This involved the application of one oil color at a time, then a thin coat of varnish, then another oil color, another coat of varnish, etc. Because Bok attempted this technique with cheap varnishes, the surfaces of many of his early paintings have cracked. The picture on page 21, circa 1938, shows clear signs of such cracking. Glazing gave an effect to Bok's work he described as "kodachromes of the impossible."[9] Like Parrish, Bok sought the effect of stained glass in his paintings.[10]

By 1939 Bok's artistic maturation was complete. The stage was now set for his burst into the professional pulp magazines, which had always been his goal. At the first World Science-Fiction Convention in July of that year, Ray Bradbury, in the presence of Erle Korshak, Mark Reinsberg, Forrest J Ackerman, and Myrtle R. Douglas, showed a portfolio of Bok's artwork to the legendary editor of *Weird Tales*, Farnsworth Wright. Wright was enthusiastic. Bok made his professional debut in the December 1939 issue of *Weird Tales* with both a cover painting and interior illustrations. Given Bok's preference for fantasy over science-fiction it seems appropriate that his debut was in a fantasy/horror magazine.[11]

The next fifteen years, for both artistry and ambition, were the apex of Bok's career. In 1939 he moved to New York and began working for the pulp magazines of which he had been a fan for so long. These years were marred, however, by constant disputes between Bok and various book and magazine editors and publishers over pay, deadlines, and artistic control. Bok was as uncompromising as his father. As a result he produced only some three hundred illustrations during his most productive years.

Of course, his methods of painting did not help matters. Bok first thoroughly read every story, and then took a great deal of time planning each picture before even beginning to paint. In an August 2, 1948 letter to Shasta Publishers (which arrived typewritten on three separate postcards) Bok discussed his problem with making a sketch rather than a finished piece:

> Number 1 (too broke to get 3 cent stamp—have cards on hand)
> Dear Mel: In my last letter to Ted I tried to explain (a) that I cannot make "rough sketches." I don't know how. I can only make FINISHED PICTURES. I have never made a rough sketch in my life, except tiny little things that nobody cud decipher save myself. My procedure on getting an order is to do a very careful outline drawing, which takes longer to do (to get composition right, & plan color-or-shading) than the actual finishing up. I spend 3 days on this layout and only 2 actually finishing it. Since pattern is my main objective in Art, and subject-matter and "finish" mere details, I cannot do "rough work"—every line must be there for a reason. Therefore, a "rough sketch" would be one of these fine-layouts—or about 3 days' work per layout—and not having my mind, you couldn't possibly see how it would look when finished; therefore you'd get an erroneous idea of the finished piece & dislike it when you saw it. I have had some very unpleasant experiences with this submission of roughs—once on a $100 job, I had to submit 7 (SEVEN) sketches—none of which were okayed, though I spent a month doing them—so that when in desperation I submitted a FINISHED PICTURE (which was at once okayed) the $100 job had

taken SIX WEEKS. When I did covers for WEIRD, I generally submitted finely-worked "sketches" which have since been sold as FINISHED PICTURES (maybe you've seen these—the 7 x 10 Horror in Glen, Bat and Sphinx covers). I learned then that other people can't understand my sketches—if I point to a blank area, saying "this will be a soft peacock blue," they yowl when they see it becuz they thought peacock blue was deep ultramarine....Also, I cannot whip up a half-dozen layouts (at about 3 days each) when only one (if any) will be acceptable)—the $15. job would thereby average out to about 15 cents per day. I sent a list of ideas to Ted in my last letter—if I had at least an idea which he liked, I could do perhaps two of them—as FINISHED pictures. But this asking me to whip up some roughs is like asking a visiting writer (say, Merritt) to sit down and whip you up a couple of short stories on the spot—he didn't write that way; neither do I draw that way. Remember, I didn't go to art school, and therefore don't work like the "average" artist. I'm living on borrowed money, cannot borrow any more, so come Aug. 15th—unless something good has turned up, I'm out on my ear, & if that happens, nobody will ever hear my name again—I'm pretty much disgusted with everything.

Well—that's it—so, if any ideas suggested in my last sound good, name the best two & I'll do them up as finished drawings. Thanks for forwarding letter, & my best to you both.

Yours,

Hannes

The glazing process, when Bok used it, was also meticulous and involved long drying of the various layers. What's more, Bok had no regular working hours. When he was interested in a job, he would work around the clock. He would not open his door to guests or even eat during these periods. Afterward he might not paint again for several days.

Another reason for Bok's modest output was his other interests: he was also a writer, lithographer, woodcarver, occult philosopher and correspondent. His written works include: "Starstone World" in *Science-Fiction Quarterly*, 1942; "The Sorcerer's Ship" in *Unknown*, December, 1942; "The Blue Flamingo", in *Startling Stories*, January, 1948; completion of A. Merritt's unfinished stories *The Fox Woman and the Blue Pagoda* and *The Black Wheel*; and a book of poetry, *Spinner of Silver and Thistle*.

Especially time-consuming was the prolific correspondence that Bok carried on throughout his life. In his biography of Bok, Emil Petaja estimated that Bok spent half of every day corresponding. Each letter he wrote was unique inasmuch as he "had his own simplified spelling and a passion for using words of his own creation with which to close each letter."[12] This correspondence may have acted as compensation for the lack of any family life on Bok's part. Bok never married and speculation exists about his sexual orientation.[13]

Despite Bok's modest production of artwork, the body of his work contains several masterpieces. The earliest one is "Ase on the Hillock" (*plate IV*) completed in 1938 and based on Grieg's, *Peer Gynt Suite*. The sketches for the piece were completed in 1936. Bok's model for the figure of Gynt's mother, Ase, was Emil Petaja's own mother, Hanna Koski Petaja. "This painting (2'x3') depicts a magnificent woman in peasant dress and shawl standing on a hillock in marshy country. There are boiling clouds in the background. The woman's skirt is blown by the wind, her eyes are turned up to defy the storm, her gnarled fingers are curled up as if to battle the elements of fate."[14] The painting shows the heavy influence of Parrish on the young Bok, from his use of glazing to the Parrish-like foliage in the background.

"Ase" was completed before Bok's professional debut in the "pulps." The first few years of working in that field (1939-1944), before the great "Powers Series," were for Bok a time of continued refinement of style. Because the pulps paid so poorly, they made less specific demands on the artist, so Bok had some freedom for stylistic experiments. On the other hand, "most artwork appearing in pulp magazines (bore) small resemblance to the original drawings."[15] This was a source of constant frustration for Bok.

In "Why Artists Go But Grey," Bok articulated the problems he encountered creating illustrations for pulp magazines. First, the "method of reproducing artwork (except in cover pictures) rules out the use of painting." That method is known as "line outs." It was "necessary to use 'line outs' in pulp magazines because of the quality of pulp paper, which is only a slight step above bathroom tissue and blotting paper. It's both too soft and coarse to take ink properly." Thus, the modern half-tone method of reproduction was not available to the pulps. The limitation of the 'line out' method was that it reproduced only pure black. "Thus, the artist if he wishes to use greys in his pictures, must simulate them, by spreading out in a white area, a lot of tiny dots or hairlines—achieving a half and half mixture, which the eye blends into an appropriate grey..." Since the method of reproduction was so crude, Bok asked rhetorically "how could you tell if the original work was good or not?"

Bok's solution to these shortcomings was to stylize his pictures to compensate for any lack of subtlety that occurred when black and white drawings were reproduced. Bok began to use line so as to create tension in a piece. Even though no overt action existed in a particular scene, through the use of lush outline curves, a feeling that movement had or was about to occur was suggested. The figures in his pieces became free flowing or fluid with exaggerated detail. In a later article Bok stated, "A factual illustration is an insult to (a reader's) intelligence. I believe that an illustration should suggest the mood and events of the story, thereby acting much the same as the 'blurb' following the title of the story. I like to make pictures... showing things not as they are... which we all know too well... but pictures of things as they might be..."[16]

By the time Bok completed "The Powers Series" in 1945, (pages 66 through 69), he had attained the ultimate refinement in his artistic technique. A series of four lithographs, "The Grey Powers," "The Powers of Darkness," "The Primal Powers," and "The Powers of Light," shows Bok at the height of his powers. By using lithography Bok avoided many of the reproduction problems inherent to the "line out" system used in the pulp field.

The figures in these pictures appear three-dimensional with well-defined musculature— "there is almost a feeling that the objects can be touched with the hands."[17] The use of line is both rhythmic and dynamic. Each picture has a total sense of balance with the figures arranged so that the direction of the viewing eye travels concentrically back to its place of beginning. The highlighting effect achieved through the range of black, grays and white is striking in the lithographs, compared to line-out reproductions of the same period. The images are sexually and anatomically suggestive: one illustration (page 66) depicts a man materializing out of a woman's thought, who is being simultaneously engulfed into her womb. In another (page 67), a man grasps a naked female form in one hand and personified male genitalia in the other. Both illustrations may reflect Bok's sexual ambivalence. This series demonstrates just how far Bok had progressed artistically from Parrish's earlier influence. The subject matter and the simple but strong use of line show the influence of Aubrey Beardsley, while the images of horror display the influence of Sidney Sime.

Bok continued making attempts to branch out of the pulp field. From January 2nd through the 13th, 1945, he showed some of his best paintings at the Ferragil Gallery, located then at 63 East 57th Street in New York. The effort was unsuccessful. It was also during this time that Bok completed writing and illustrating A. Merritt's two unfinished manuscripts mentioned earlier. That experience, however, was an unpleasant one for Bok, since he received no payment from it.

With the publication of his *Skull-Face and Others* dust jacket (Arkham House, 1946) illustrating a Robert E. Howard story and his *Slaves of Sleep* dust jacket (Shasta, 1949) illustrating an L. Ron Hubbard novel,[18] Bok entered a new phase in his professional and artistic career. No longer was he illustrating only pulp magazines, but hardcover books for specialty presses as well. One of these, Shasta Publishers, spent large sums of money developing color separations to lavishly reproduce the illustrations on their books' dust jackets. This resulted in some of the most accurate and dramatic reproductions of Bok originals ever accomplished.

In *Skull-Face* (page 9) we see the same graceful flowing use of line and balance of composition used in "The Powers"; however, the images are now in exquisite color. The only resemblance to Parrish is the glazed blue background. The figures are totally stylized and in no way realistic. *Slaves of Sleep* (page 2) is similar to *Skull-Face* with its vivid blue background and repetition of various fairy-tale-like symbols—a castle and a sorcerer's ship. The floating woman has an almost ethereal effect, while the action of the picture "is frozen into eternally posed choreography."[19]

In the Fantasy/Horror field an artist is only as good as his monsters. Bok's monsters were second to none.[20] The greatest is probably found in the 1950 black and white illustration for the H.P. Lovecraft story "Pickman's Model," (page 71). The juxtaposition of a huge, gruesome face with a human torso gives the picture an eerie, otherworldly feeling. Its eyes, the most prominent white objects in the picture, seem almost ablaze. The size of the monster, in comparison with the pathetic human it holds in its hand, gives it an almost deity-like presence.

Ironically in 1952, when Bok received the highest honor bestowed for science-fiction illustration, the first Hugo art award, he was also beginning to phase himself out of the field.[21] Bok had become disgusted with the low pay offered by the magazines. More importantly he had become disgusted with the fans themselves. "What really finished me up was the types of persons I met in fantasy circles. Usually thick-spectacled 17 year-olds who thought they owned you because they'd done you the favor of buying a magazine. I've had 'fans' barge in on me at all hours of the day and night (one at 4:00 a.m.), they snoop into my closets and dresser drawers, read my mail if I don't snatch it away from them ('Oh, I see you got a letter from Henry Kuttner! What does he say?') and get real ugly when you won't give them an original off your walls, simply because they like it."[22] The boy Wayne Woodard, who had started as a fan and transformed himself into the professional artist Hannes Bok, had now turned against the fantasy art field itself.

Further complications existed. With the advent of the atomic bomb and the end of the second world war, changes were occurring in the science-fiction/fantasy field. The public was enamored of technology and the genre was turning away from Bok's forte which was fantasy. By 1954 the pulp era was ending. Fantasy magazines such as *Weird Tales*, where Bok had made his debut, were dying with it. Bok's job market was drying up. Bok was further handicapped because unlike some of his contemporaries, he had never become identified with any one author or pulp magazine—which might have helped pull him through such a difficult period.[23]

Eventually, after years of frustration and neglect Bok became a defeatist. The man whom friends had once described as elfin, whose earlier art work had displayed so much whimsy, was now a bitter cynic.

Bok turned increasingly to mysticism and occult philosophy. "As the years wore on and bitterness wore deep ruts into his soul, as he retreated more and more into his shell, he turned for some meaning in life to the mystical."[24] Perhaps this was an effort to find in the real world the same type of harmony that his art portrayed. At the same time Bok's artwork took on a mystical dimension. He began painting madonnas and mandalas. To support himself during his last ten years Bok did some cover illustrations for the occultist works of Dion Fortune.[25] He also worked on art of his own interest, such as mask making.

The last great farewell piece of fantasy illustration Bok did was "A Rose for Ecclesiastes" for a Roger Zelazny story. This painting appeared as the cover of the November, 1963, issue of *The Magazine of Fantasy and Science-Fiction* (reproduced from the original painting, pages 86-87). "Rose" is an other-worldly mystical mood piece that seems to portray the phase of life Bok was experiencing. In this painting, more than in any other, he seems to be after life's spiritual principle. Everything in the picture—the use of perspective, the maidens' music, the manner of holding the rose, the gaze of the rock's face—seems to direct the viewer toward some metaphysical enigma. Bok described the piece in process: "got carried away and designed it as if it were 11x16 feet, instead of inches. If it comes out as expected, it'll be a riot of reds and blue-greens, be as enamel-surfaced as a Dali original."[26]

On April 11, 1964, at 49 years of age, Bok died of an apparent heart attack. After unsuccessfully trying to reach him, a neighbor became suspicious and called the police. When they opened his door Bok had been dead for several days. "He died alone at night, unnoticed,"[27] a recluse except for his beautiful artwork. If not for the efforts of a friend, Clarence Peacock, Bok's artwork would probably have been carted away by the building's superintendent to the nearest garbage dump.

This volume is an attempt to acquaint a larger public with the body of his work.

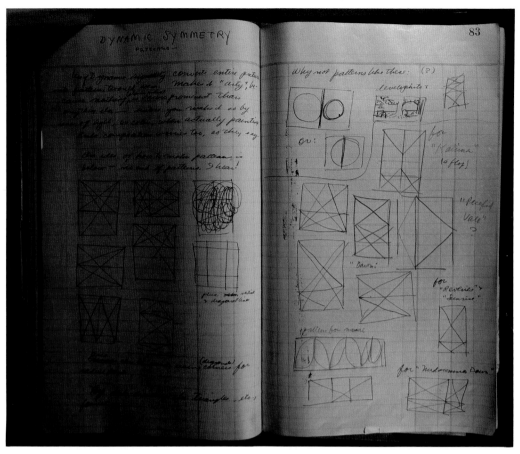

plate I

plate II

plate III

plate IV

Notes

1. Howard Pyle received a salary of $36,000 a year in 1906 as art director for *McClure's,* which was not exorbitant in those days for a man in his position. Hannes Bok was paid an average of $5.00 per picture in 1940 and $20.00 per picture in 1951. He estimated that a hack illustrator whipping out pictures in the pulps in 1951 could earn $1,500 per year. See Hannes Bok, "Why Artists Go But Grey," *The Big O,* Les & Es Cole and Lee Jacobs eds., August, 1951.

2. According to Emil Petaja, Bok's biographer, the first known appearance of Hans Bok on artwork is dated December 1934–January 1935, *Fantasy Magazine,* linoleum cut cover of *Cosmos.*

3. Lowndes, Robert A. W. "Memories of Hannes Bok." Gerry de la Ree, ed., page 20. Lowndes referred to "pseudo namesake" but did not confirm derivation of Bok from Bach.

4. Hannes Bok, "A Brief Autobiography," *Bizarre,* January 1941, reprinted in *Bok (A Tribute),* Gerry de la Ree, ed., Saddle River, NJ, page 18.

5. A tradition of study and influence between Pyle, Parrish and Bok exists. Parrish, after his graduation from Haverford, "studied for two years at the Pennsylvania Academy of the Fine Arts and attended some classes of Howard Pyle's at the Drexel Institute. (It is reported that Pyle, after an examination of Parrish's portfolio, announced there was nothing more he could teach the young artist, recommending only that Parrish develop a more individual style in his work.)" Susan Mayer, *America's Great Illustrators,* (New York: Galahad, 1987), page 116.

6. Based on a letter Parrish wrote to Bok's friend Franklin Dietz on May 8, 1984, some writers have speculated that Bok never visited Parrish. In the letter, Parrish stated that he never met Bok but did receive letters from him. However, this letter was written when Parrish was 94 years old and perhaps somewhat short of memory. These writers have not taken into account the two valuable Parrish sketches mentioned below or the personally inscribed books from Parrish to Bok which exist. Finally in an unpublished interview conducted by art historian Robert Weinberg with fantasy artist Edd Cartier in 1990, Cartier mentioned that Bok definitely visited Parrish at least once and recalled some details of that meeting as described to him by Bok.

7. These notebooks are accompanied with a letter of provenance from Bok's friend Jack Gaughan stating that he recovered them from Bok's apartment upon his death.

8. Coy Ludwig, *Maxfield Parrish,* (New York: Watson-Gupthill, 1972), page 128.

9. Hannes Bok, "Hannes Bok Looks at Fantasy Art and Illustration," *The Fanscient* 12, Donald Day, ed. 1951.

10. A number of Bok's works have been examined and treated by the Florida paper conservator Maury Barlow Pepin. In the process, information was gleaned about Bok's materials and their handling. Mr. Pepin's notes include the following information:

> Bok did thumb-nail sketches in pencil and artist's crayon on newsprint stock. A few of these have survived in his spiral-bound portfolios. Like those of many artists who work strictly for publication, most of Bok's finished black-and-white drawings and color paintings were done on commercial illustration board. This is a very flat, tough material which can withstand the repeated handling involved in the printing production process. Illustration board generally consists of an 1/8-

inch-thick base of grey or brown solid cardboard stock, with a thin layer of smooth or slightly-textured white artists' paper factory-mounted on it.

Bok painted and drew on boards with either Strathmore cold-pressed kid bristol paper, or the smoother hot-pressed plate bristol. These hard-surfaced papers take inks and water-based media very well, and allow for complete control of surface texture by the artist. The paintings examined by the conservator were later works done in mixed materials, combining dry pastel and opaque gouaches with the oil-based fixative media and varnishes Bok used to make his glazes. Judging by their resistance to fading over fifty years time and more, the pigments Bok used were of very high quality.

Bok didn't trust the entire reproduction process to the publisher's staff. He sometimes worked by hand on transparent sheets of acetate, creating overlays to give the exact background effects he desired. An impressive example of one of Bok's "Kodachromes of the impossible" is an entire four-color printing separation hand-painted by the artist on clear acetate. The effect is like looking at a stained-glass window.

The physical condition of surviving illustrations is what one might expect in what was basically an industrial situation. The two-inch margin outside the painting itself is often covered with printer's marks and notes in crayon or grease pencil. Tapes and adhesives of different kinds were used to hold the work for photography. Although these are interesting as records of the process, many of the materials, especially the tapes, have caused staining and other preservation problems. The art paper of the illustration boards is very dense and has so far resisted acidic stain-through from the mounting cardboard underneath. Preservation of such original illustration-board works for posterity will eventually require removal of the acidic cardboard backings from the facing paper. M. Barlow Pepin, 783 S. Atmore Circle, Deltona, Florida 32725.

11. After Bok joined a New York group of fans called the Futurians in 1941, he met a number of future editors and writers who began commissioning him to do more science-fiction artwork. Bok, however, was never really very comfortable with science-fiction. In an August 23, 1944 letter to his friend Rah Hoffman, Bok stated; "Nope I didn't send you a space ship because I hate them. I'm lousy on machinery anyways. I hate things mechanical (unless they're record players, typers, etc.) But space ships to be acceptable, have to look like phallic tin cans, if I must draw em, I'd rather draw lovely fanciful ones."

12. Gerry de la Ree, "With Snarpps and Strazzen Dilfers", *Luna* 4, Franklin M. Dietz, Jr., ed., Page 7.

13. An extensive love correspondence exists between Bok and the science-fiction writer Henry Hasse. Speculation also exists that Bok was romantically involved with one of several women and, thus, perhaps, bisexual.

14. Emil Petaja, "The Life and Legend of Hannes Bok", in *And Flight of Angels*, Emil Petaja, ed. (Bokanalia Memorial Foundation, 1968), page 30.

15. Hannes Bok, "Why Artists Go But Grey," *The Big O*, Les and Es Cole & Lee Jacobs, eds., August, 1951, page 22.

16. Hannes Bok, "Hannes Bok Looks At Fantasy Art and Illustration," *The Fanscient* 12, *ibid.*, and also reprinted in *And Flight of Angels*, *ibid.*, pages 114, 117.

17. Morris Scott Dollens quoted by Darrell Richardson in "The People Who Make Other Worlds," (Hannes Bok) Ray Palmer, ed. *Other Worlds*, April, 1952, page 159.

18. *Skull-Face and Others*, (Sauk City, WI: Arkham House, 1946) and *Slaves of Sleep*, (Chicago: Shasta Publishers, 1949).

19. Ben Indick, "Yizgitzers: A Memory," in *Bok (A Tribute)*, ed. by Gerry de la Ree, page 53.

20. Sometimes, however, the reproductions did not do Bok's monsters justice. For example, Bok commented on the final *Who Goes There?* jacket cover, (page 4), that "As for the jacket, I'm not so happy about it. I'd rather have had the thing all blue, instead of with the comic-book additions of red spots. The scarlet lipstick, rouged nipples and painted nails of the tailed men are just too too sweet. All he needs now is earrings, a bracelet, necklace, and a treble voice." Shasta Publishers, Unpublished Hannes Bok correspondence, circa 1947-1949.

21. Actually he shared the award with one of his contemporaries, Ed Emsh (formerly Ed Emshwiller).

22. Emil Petaja, *And Flights of Angels, ibid.*, page 57.

23. J. Allen St. John, another fantasy artist, for example, was intimately identified with Edgar Rice Burroughs. Though he originally illustrated Burroughs novels in the 1920s, he was commissioned again in the late 1940s to illustrate previously unpublished manuscripts for the magazine *Amazing Stories* because the reading public identified him so closely with Burroughs' work.

24. Emil Petaja, *And Flights of Angels, ibid.*, page 66.

25. For example, Dion Fortune, *The Esoteric Orders and Their Works* (St. Paul, MN: Llewlyn Publishers).

26. Emil Petaja, "Hannes Bok On Creative Art," *Trumpet*, Tom Reamy & Alex Eisenstein eds., 1969, page 4. The actual magazine cover illustration of the original "Rose" painting reversed all the images in the picture from left to right.

27. Emil Petaja, *A Memorial Portfolio: Hannes Bok* (Bokanalia Memorial Foundation, 1970), page 2.

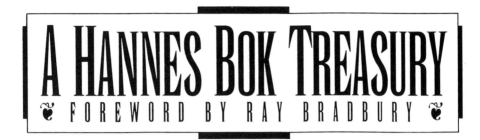

A HANNES BOK TREASURY

FOREWORD BY RAY BRADBURY

Slaves of Sleep, by L. Ron Hubbard, 1949. Dust jacket reproduced from the collection of Erle Melvin and Stephen Dedalus Korshak.

4

Who Goes There?, by John Campbell, 1947. Dust jacket reproduced from the collection of Erle Melvin and Stephen Dedalus Korshak.

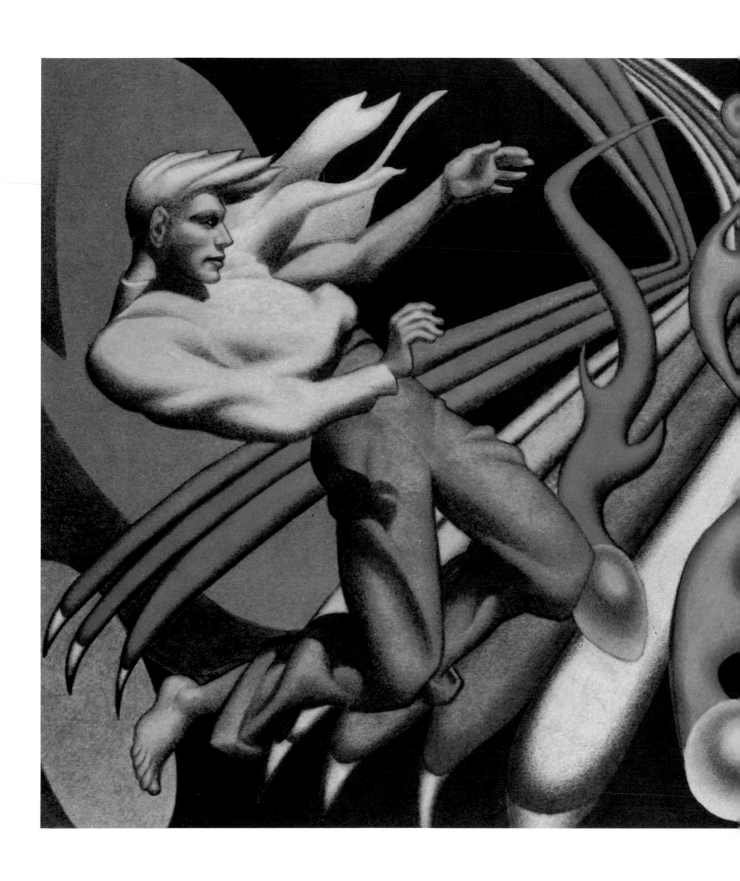

The Wheels of If, by L. Sprague deCamp, 1947. Dust jacket reproduced from the collection of Erle Melvin and Stephen Dedalus Korshak.

Illustration for *The Enchanted Castle*, 1946.

Illustration for *Skull-Face and Others*, by Robert E. Howard, 1946. From the collection of Gene Nigra.

Illustration for "Terminal Quest," by Poul Anderson, 1951.

Illustration for *The Enchanted City*, from Emil Petaja's *A Memorial Portfolio: Hannes Bok*. From the collection of Dr. Stuart Schiff.

Illustration for "The Weapon," by H. B. Ogden.
[*opposite*: Illustration for *The Cat God's Captive*. From the collection of Gene Nigra.]

Black and white illustration.

Illustration for *Other Worlds*, January 1953, (back cover). From the collection of Robert Weinberg.

Illustration for *The Fox Woman and The Blue Pagoda*, by A. Merritt and Hannes Bok, 1946.

Unpublished illustration from the collection of Forrest J Ackerman.

Illustration for "Altars of Patagonia," 1946.

Illustration for *Space Science Fiction*, March 1953. From the collection of Gene Nigra.

Black and white illustration.

Illustration from the collection of Ray Bradbury.

Black and white illustration from the collection of Erle Melvin and Stephen Dedalus Korshak.

Illustration for "Alien Rides Under a Golden Sky," 1936. Courtesy of Illustration House Gallery.

Illustration from Emil Petaja's *A Memorial Portfolio: Hannes Bok.*

Illustration for "Outpost of the Eons," by Dirk Wylie and Frederik Pohl, 1943.

Unpublished illustration from the collection of Erle Melvin and Stephen Dedalus Korshak.

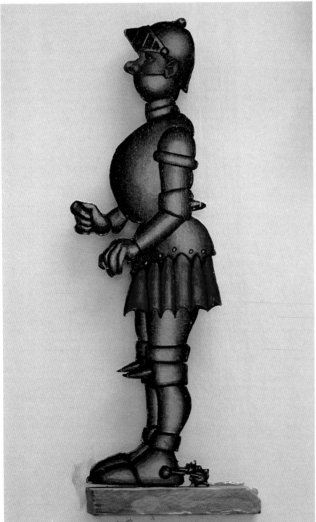

Various woodcarvings from the collection of Howard and Jane Frank.

Illustration from the collection of Gene Nigra.

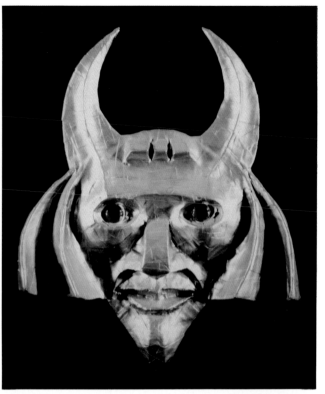

Paper maché masks. From the collection of Gene Nigra (upper) and Erle Melvin and Stephen Dedalus Korshak (lower).

Costume design, unpublished, signed to Dunninger, from the collection of Gerry de la Ree.

Sidewise in Time, by Murray Leinster. Dust jacket reproduced from the collection of Erle Melvin and Stephen Dedalus Korshak.

Illustration for "The Sorcerer's Ship," 1942 (written by Hannes Bok)

Illustration for "The Sorcerer's Ship," 1942 (written by Hannes Bok)

Illustration for "The Sorcerer's Ship," 1942 (written by Hannes Bok)

37

Illustration for "Circe," 1946.

38

From the collection of Ray Bradbury.

Illustration for "By What Mystic Mooring," by Frank Owen, 1941.

Illustration from *Famous Fantastic Mysteries*, 1949.

Illustration from *Famous Fantastic Mysteries*, 1949.

Black and white illustration.

Illustration for "Out of the Storm," by William Hope Hodgson. From the collection of Robert Lesser.

Illustration for "The Sorcerer's Ship," 1942 (written by Hannes Bok).

Illustration for "After a Million Years," *Weird Tales*, 1946. From the collection of Robert Weinberg.

Illustration for "The Yellow Sign," by Robert W. Chambers, 1943.

Illustration for "Seven Out of Time," by Arthur Leo Zagat, 1949.

Black and white illustration.
[*opposite*: From the collection of Gene Nigra.]

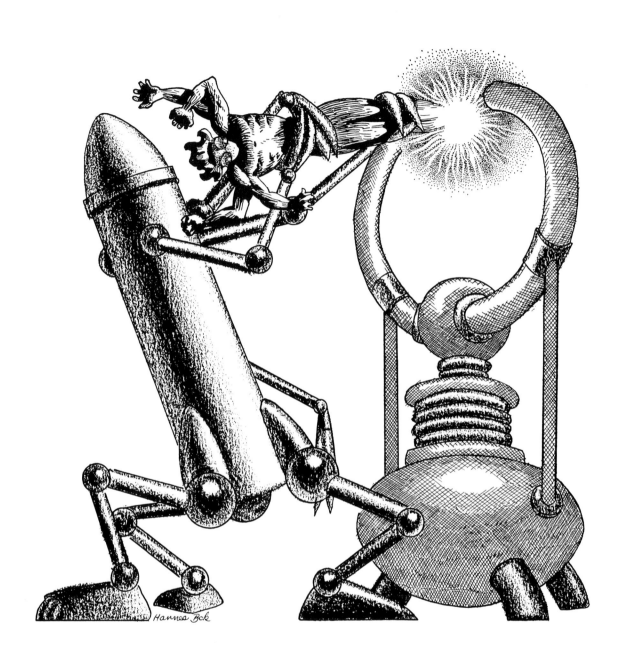

Illustration for "The Cat-Men of Aemt," by Neil J. Jones, 1940.

Illustration for "The Robot God," by Ray Cummings, 1941. From the collection of Gene Nigra. [*following*: Illustration for "TheCity from the Sea," by Edmund Hamilton, *Weird Tales*, 1940. From the collection of Erle Melvin and Stephen Dedalus Korshak.]

The House on the Borderland, by William Hope Hodgson. Reproduced from the collection of Erle Melvin and Stephen Dedalus Korshak
[*previous page*: Illustration for "The Horror in the Glenn," by Clyde Irvine, *Weird Tales*, 1940. From the collection of Gene Nigra.]

Black and white illustration.

Prometheus Bound, unpublished Bookplate, commissioned by Shasta Publishers.

Illustration for "Nightmare," 1939.

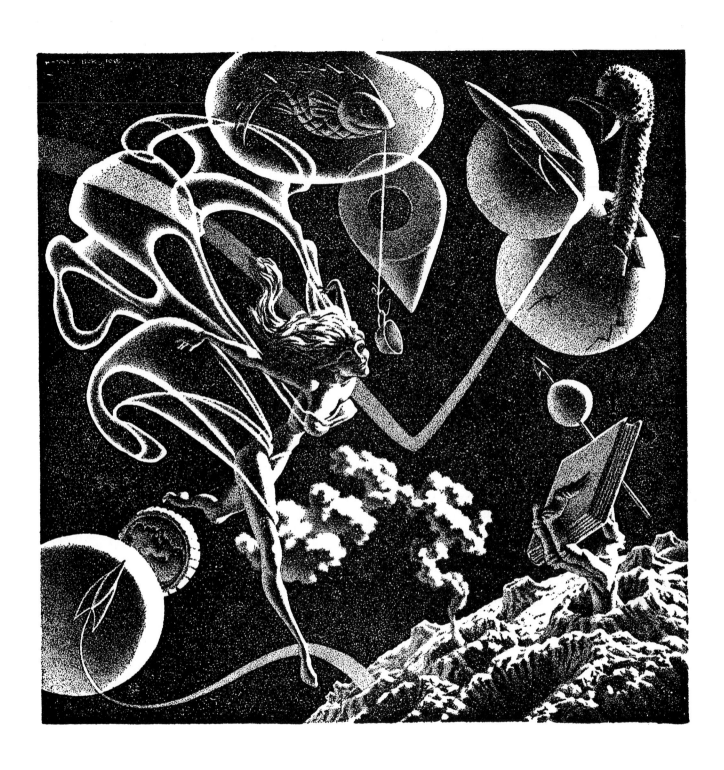

Black and white illustration.

Illustration for "Mantle of Frosty Stars," 1949.

Illustration for *Pendulum*, by Ray Bradbury and Henry Hasse, 1941.

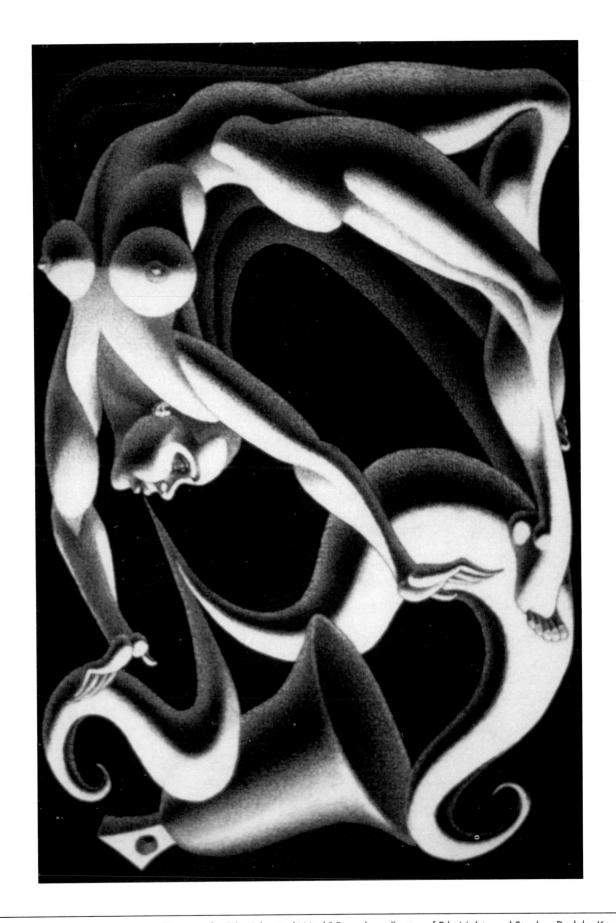

Illustration for "The Educated Wind." From the collection of Erle Melvin and Stephen Dedalus Korshak.

"The Powers of Light," 1945, Lithograph.

"The Powers of Darkness," 1945, Lithograph.

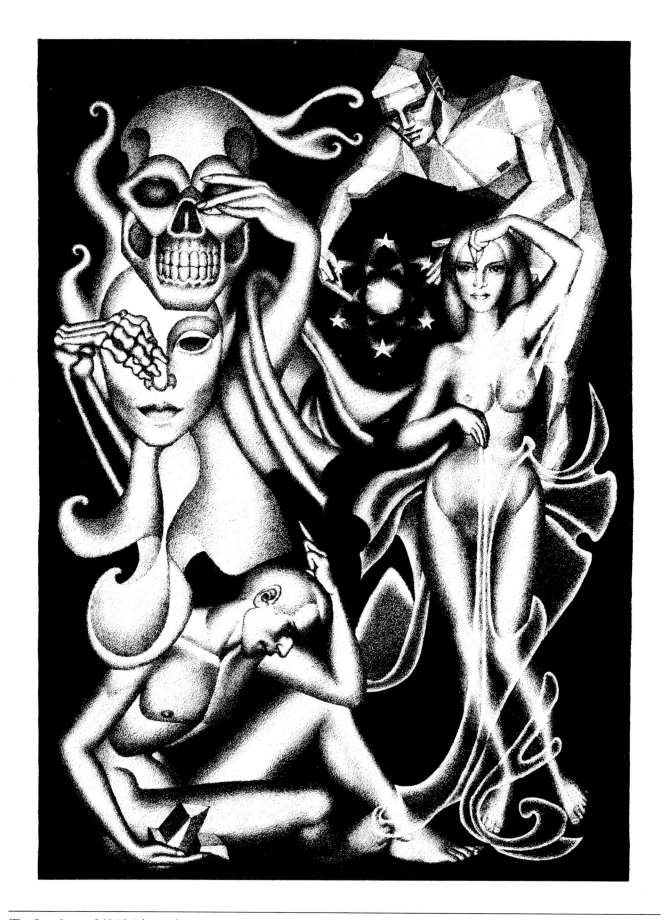

"The Grey Powers," 1945, Lithograph.

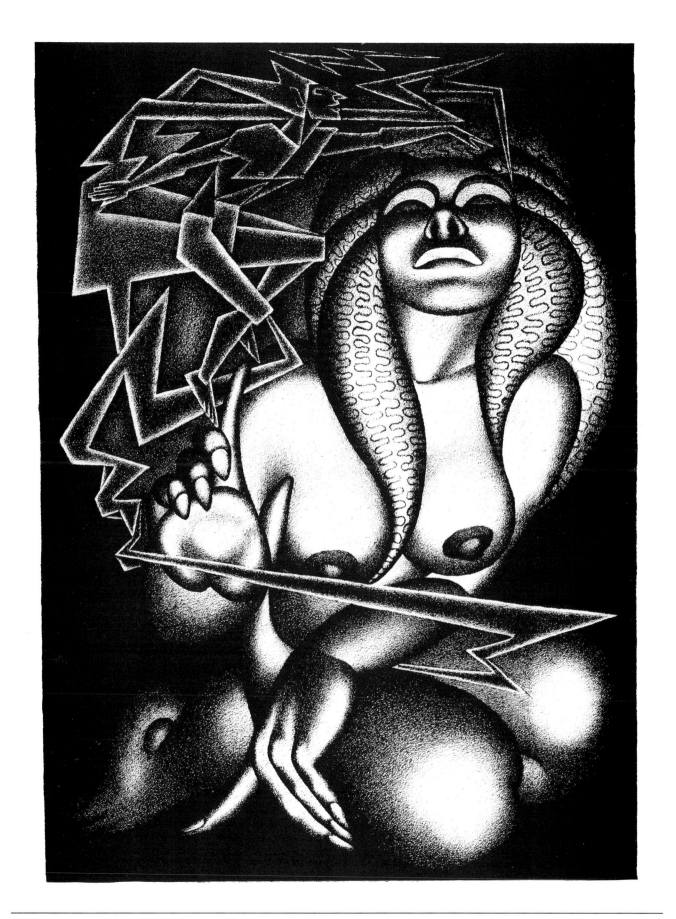

"The Primal Powers," 1945, Lithograph.

Mandala, 1956.

Illustration for "Pickman's Model," by H.P. Lovecraft, 1951. From the collection of Gene Nigra.

Illustration for "War God's Gamble," by Harry Walton, 1951. From the collection of Gene Nigra.

Illustration for "Song of the Sirens," by Edward Lucas White, 1951.

Illustration for "Journey's End," by Walter Kubilius, 1943. From the collection of Ronald Clyne.

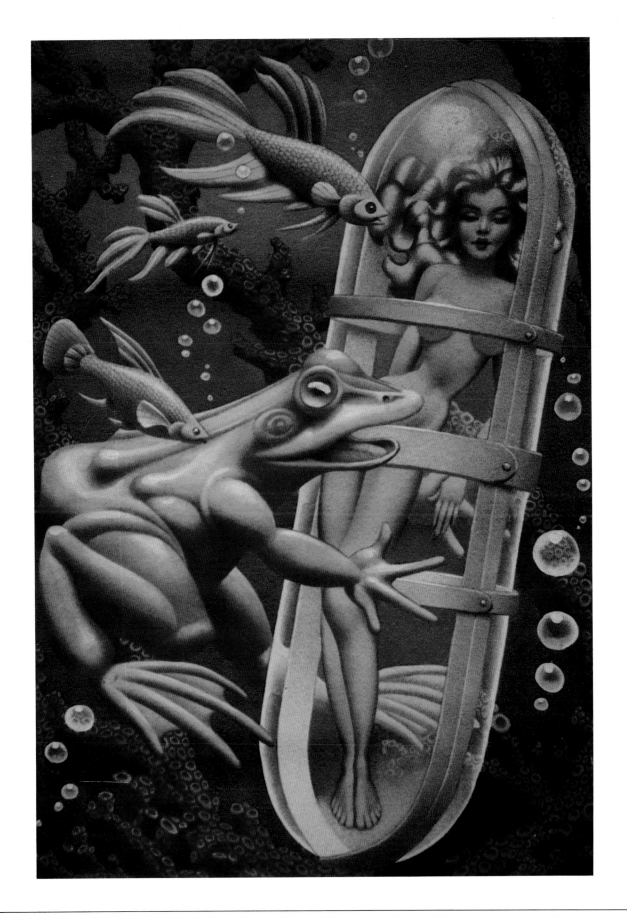

Illustration for "Red Coral," by Ray Palmer, *Other Worlds*, 1951. From the collection of Gerry de la Ree.

Black and white illustration.

Black and white illustration.

Illustration from *Famous Fantastic Mysteries*.

Illustration for "Oblivion Quest," by Wilbur S. Peacock, 1951. From the collection of Erle Melvin and Stephen Dedalus Korshak.

Black and white illustration.

Illustration for "Hell's Angels," by Robert Bloch, *Imagination*, 1951. From the collection of Gene Nigra.

Unpublished painting from the collection of Gerry de la Ree.

Illustration for "The Enchanted River," by Dorothy Quick, 1942.

Black and white illustration.

Cover illustration for "It Went Thataway," by Harvey Frey, *Marvel Science Fiction*, August 1951. From the collection of
Erle Melvin and Stephen Dedalus Korshak.

Illustration for "A Rose for Ecclesiates." From the collection of Erle Melvin and Stephen Dedalus Korshak.

Bibliography

Bok, Hannes. "Hannes Bok Looks At Fantasy and Illustration," *The Fanscient 12*, Donald Day, ed., 1951.

———. "Hannes Looks at Bok," *Wastebasket 4*, Vernon L. McCain, ed., 1954.

———. Unpublished Notebooks, circa 1932-1935.

———. "Why Artists Go But Grey," *The Big O*, Les and Es Cole & Lee Jacobs, eds., August 1951.

Brooks, C.W. *The Revised Hannes Bok Checklist*. Baltimore: T-K Graphics, 1973.

Carr, Terry. "Entropy Reprints: Hannes Bok." *Beabohema 17*, Frank Lunney, ed., August 1971.

de la Ree, Gerry. *A Hannes Bok Sketch Book*. Gerry de la Ree and Gene Nigra, eds., Saddle River, N.J. 1976.

———. "About Hannes Bok." *Beauty and the Beast: The Art of Hannes Bok*. Gerry de la Ree, ed., Saddle River, NJ: de la Ree, 1978.

———. "With Snarpps and Strazzendilfers." *Luna 4*, Franklin M. Dietz, Jr., ed., 1965.

———. *Bok (A Tribute)*, Gerry de la Ree, ed., 1974.

Dietz, Jr., Franklin M. "Hister." *Luna 4*, Franklin M. Dietz, Jr., ed., 1965.

Gaughan, Jack. "Hannes Bok." *And Flights of Angels*, Emil Petaja, ed., Bokanalia Memorial Foundation, 1968.

Hoffman, Rah. Unpublished Hannes Bok Correspondence, circa 1944.

Indick, Ben. "The Remembered Elf." *And Flights of Angels*, Emil Petaja, ed., Bokanalia Memorial Foundation, 1968.

———. "Hannes Bok: Artist and Man," *Chacal 1*, Byron Roark, ed., 1976.

Knight, Damon. *The Futurians*. New York: John Day, 1977.

Lee, Godfrey. "Hannes Bok." *And Flights of Angels*. Emil Petaja, ed., Bokanalia Memorial Foundation, 1968.

Ludwig, Coy. *Maxfield Parrish*. New York: Watson-Guptill, 1973.

Lupoff, Richard A. "The Hermit." *Luna 4*, Franklin M. Dietz, Jr., ed., 1965.

Meyer, Susan. *America's Great Illustrators*. New York: Galahad, 1987.

Parrish, Maxfield. "A Letter." *Luna 4*, Franklin M. Dietz, Jr., ed., 1965.

Petaja, Emil. "The Life and Legend of Hannes Bok." *And Flights of Angles*. Emil Petaja, ed., Bokanalia Memorial Foundation, 1968.

———. "Hannes Bok on Creative Art." *Trumpet 9*, Tom Reamy & Alex Eisenstein, eds., 1969.

———. *A Memorial Portfolio: Hannes Bok*. Bokanalia Memorial Foundation, 1970.

———. *The Hannes Bok Memorial Showcase of Fantasy Art*. Emil Petaja, ed. San Francisco, CA, 1974.

Reed, Walt, and Reed, Roger. *The Illustrator in America 1880-1980: A Century of Illustrations*. New York: The Society of Illustrators, 1984.

Richardson, Darrell C., "The People Who Make Other Worlds." Hannes Bok, Ray Palmer, ed., *Other Worlds*, April, 1952.

Shasta Publishers. Unpublished Hannes Bok correspondence, circa 1947- 1949.

Skeeters, Paul W. *Sidney Sime: Master of Fantasy*. Pasadena, CA: Ward Ritchie, 1978.

Walker, R.A. *The Best of Beardsley*. U.S.A.: Excalibur, 1948.

Warner, Harry Jr., *All Our Yesterdays*. Chicago: Advent Publishers, 1969.

Weinberg, Robert. *A Biographical Dictionary of Science Fiction and Fantasy Artists*. Westport, CT: Greenwood Press, 1988.

Wollheim, Donald A. "A Non-Eulogy." *And Flights of Angels*. Emil Petaja, ed., Bokanalia Memorial Foundation, 1968.

Wright, Rosco. "Our Bok." *Beyond*.

PHOTOGRAPHY CREDITS